I0177371

Mindful Moments:

Everyday
Mindfulness
for
Real
People

By Haven E. Carter

Copyright © 2017 Haven E. Carter

All rights reserved

Printed in the United States of America

No part of this book may be reproduced in any form or by any means electronic or mechanical, without permission in writing from the publisher.

Edited by Martha Hayes, dedicatededitor.com
Cover design by Michael Corvin,
http://furyowl.wix.com/corvindesign
Book design by Polgarus Studio, polgarusstudio.com

Carter, Haven E.
Mindful Moments: Everyday Mindfulness for Real People
ISBN: 978-0-9986768-1-4 (ebook)
ISBN: 978-0-9986768-0-7 (print)

This book is dedicated to my teachers.

"Everyone is my teacher. Some I seek. Some I subconsciously attract. Often I learn simply by observing others. Some may be completely unaware that I'm learning from them, yet I bow deeply in gratitude."

Eric Allen

Contents

Introduction

This book is intended to provide little suggestions or reminders of how we might live a more mindful life in moment by moment awareness throughout each day, from the time we wake up in the morning until we fall asleep each night. Mindful living will bring calmness, peace, and more space in our lives for the moments that bring us pleasure. Yes, mindfulness will bring more pleasure into our lives.

Do you jump out of bed at the scream of the alarm to race through your day at breakneck speed, peering over your reading glasses to check the weather forecast, email, or Facebook while brushing your teeth? Is the TV blaring, coffee percolating, and the dog whining to go out while you wonder, *How will it all get done? Where is the time going?*

Do you race to work or the gym or wherever and wonder, *Why am I always running around behind the eight ball while the to-do list gets longer and the demands become more impossible to meet?*

Would you like the world to slow down so you can enjoy the ride? Smell the roses once in a while? How about all the while?

Mindfulness slows us down and makes us aware that our life is a journey, there is no final destination, and we can go with the flow and relish each experience. When practicing mindfulness, we turn inward to witness ourselves without judgment, we hold a space of loving presence, we are open and receptive to learn and receive, we accept and delight in sensation and mystery, and we feel what we feel without a need to explain it.

My mindfulness practice helps me to recognize and appreciate the beauty and art in all things, to open my heart with love and compassion for all beings in the face of fear, anger, greed and ignorance, and to accept myself as no different than all others. We are all the same and we all want the same thing—to love and be loved and to no longer suffer. It's a practice. I certainly don't get it "right" all the time or even most of the time. But when I do, it's sweet.

Mindfulness is paying attention to the here and now, being aware of the present moment in the present moment. My teachers and others define mindfulness more eloquently than I:

"Practicing mindfulness is setting the intention to pay attention, sustaining that attention again and again until eventually we gain a heightened sense of awareness of all around us." **Dr. Ranga Premaratna, Reiki Jin Kei Do Lineage Head, Master, and Teacher**

"Take a walk with no destination and you will begin to understand mindfulness." **Teijo Munnich, Soto Zen Monk**

"Mindfulness is the energy of attention. It is the capacity in each of us to be present one hundred percent to what is happening within and around us." **Thich Nhat Hanh, Vietnamese Buddhist Zen master, poet, scholar, and peace activist.**

"Mindfulness, or attention, on the other hand, has a magical aspect that gives vitality. I am speaking of *pure* attention—without judgment or advice.... To pay attention means to be awake, thus to be aware of what is right in front of us.... Attention is a form of kindness, and lack of attention is the greatest form of rudeness.... Inattention is cold and hard. Attention is warm and caring. It makes our best possibilities flower." **Piero Ferrucci, psychotherapist and philosopher.**

How is not paying attention to ourselves the ultimate in rudeness? It all begins with us. Paying attention to ourselves is fundamental for loving-kindness. As we pay attention to ourselves, we are able to pay better attention to others. As we begin to treat ourselves, our bodies, our emotions, and our thoughts with kindness and compassion, we also begin to treat others with loving-kindness.

This book is about doing little things every day that will help you pay attention to yourself and after that, you will find it's a pleasure and a joy to pay attention to others with love, compassion, and without judgment.

I recommended you read this book in bits. Yes, it's a small book. Read it a chapter or a few paragraphs at a time to allow the information to sink in before moving to the next part. Take your time.

Let's begin.

Chapter One
Mindful Mornings

Awaken slowly in a lovely, even, and joyful manner. How?

Before you retire, set your alarm to play pleasing music or sounds. When the alarm sounds in the morning, it will not jar your nervous system. Instead, calming tones gently nudge you awake.

Better yet, go to bed early and allow yourself to wake up in your natural time. If you don't know how much sleep you need to feel truly rested, experiment. Some people function fine on seven hours. However, if they sleep seven and a half or eight hours, they will feel and perform better. My body and my mind love eight or nine hours. After a couple nights of nine hours of restful sleep, I'll get on a schedule of sleeping eight hours. After I pull a late night, I begin the process again.

Discover how much sleep your body wants.

When you awaken, lie in bed and listen to the sounds and silences of the music and of your home, the gentle stirring of nature coming alive again after a night of slumber. Pay attention.

Nestle yourself in the sheets and feel the blankets against your skin. Observe any sensations. Gently stretch your body, bones, joints, and muscles in all directions.

Ask yourself, *How does my body feel this morning?* Stretch again and feel your skin, your muscles, your joints, your bones, your connective tissue all moving and rousing together.

Yawn.

Lengthen your whole body and yawn again with more enthusiasm. Imitate your cat or dog. Imagine how a wild animal might arch, round, extend, and reach when it wakes up in the wild. Be the wild lion, tiger, or bear. Play.

Yawn again. Yawn louder this time. Don't be afraid to make noise.

I like to wake up each of my thirteen joints one at a time. Roll, bend, and flex your ankles, knees, hips. Spiral your wrists. Bend and flex your elbows. Roll your shoulders in one direction and then the other, and alternate them from the left to the right. Undulate your spine in and out, to the left and right, in every direction. Elongate your bones and muscles. Move all thirteen joints at the same time, juicing up your cartilage, your bones and muscles too. This process is from Nia, a beautiful, conscious movement practice.

If you don't sleep well at night, consider redefining your bedroom space. Scientists reveal adults who save their bedrooms only for sleep and sex enjoy better sleep.

What about better sex? Do your own research. Move the TV out of the bedroom.

In fact, move all your electronics out of the bedroom. Use a battery-operated clock or place your morning wake-up device in an adjacent room. Electronics and the lights emitted from them in our bedrooms upset our internal circadian rhythms, meaning our sleep cycles are disrupted which can affect our health, weight, productivity, mindfulness, relationships, consciousness, and more.

If you can, find a quiet spot first thing in the morning and sit in stillness for twenty minutes. If not twenty minutes, start by sitting for at least five minutes each morning. Build up to ten minutes over the course of a few weeks. Consistently increase the time to fifteen minutes and, in your own time, work your way up to twenty minutes each morning.

The more time you set aside to sit in stillness with your breath or meditate each morning, the more you will benefit and the more time and space you will create in your life. You will gain real time. You will have more time and energy to focus on those things that are important to you, and you will begin to prioritize and say "no" to those less important matters. You will become more attentive, more mindful.

Remember to take a few minutes throughout your day to sit in stillness. Two minutes before an important phone call or meeting can make a huge difference in your attitude, perspective, and outcome of the call or meeting. In this quiet time, you'll focus on your breath, calm your nervous system, and you may also visualize the meeting or phone call as a win-win. At the very least, you will have an open mind and heart during the encounter.

Does this sound overwhelming? Then start with three conscious breaths several times a day. Sit and inhale deeply through your nose. Allow a normal pause before you slowly and completely exhale through your mouth. Notice the rise and fall of your belly as you inhale and exhale, the expansion and contraction of your chest, and the coolness of the air as it enters your nostrils and the warmth as it exits. These aspects of your breath, these subtleties, will support your ability to calm your mental chatter, quiet your mind, and relax, rejuvenate, and energize your whole being.

Should a strong unwelcome emotion threaten to overtake you, take three conscious breaths and allow yourself a moment to feel the feelings, not squash them. Research has determined it takes 90 seconds for an emotional wave to wash over us and lessen or completely dissipate. After the emotional wave has washed over you, you will be able to thoughtfully respond—not react—and continue to create what you want.

My teachers emphasize that meditation and mindfulness require dedication, repetition, and patience. I like to add that compassion and a sense of humor help too. I find bringing self-compassion and humor is imperative for me to continually "begin again." I bring them every morning, noon, and night to handle the crazy thoughts, ideas, and sensations that distract me.

Finding your *spot* to sit is important. I believe picking your spot helps with commitment and repetition. Having a specific meditation place encourages your meditation practice to develop into a part of your daily life, a natural behavior of your mindful life. Just as you have a place where you eat your meals, park your car, read your book, exercise, and watch TV, pick a specific location where you sit in stillness and meditate. Some people create altars while others simply enjoy decorating a corner or favorite setting with candles, photographs, flowers, plants, symbols, statues, or other items. You can have a specific locale where you put a comfortable pillow or chair and light a candle, set a timer, and sit. Imagine opening your eyes after sitting in stillness. What is the first thing you want to see? Pick that spot. Remember, you can move it around until it feels like the perfect fit. Consider how an animal walks around searching for just the right spot before it lies down to rest. You can do the same.

As you prepare for your day, get in touch with your five senses—touch, taste, smell, sound, and sight. Caress, savor, sniff, and investigate the soaps, lotions, and pastes as well as cloths, towels, and brushes around you.

Are your soaps and lotions alluring and agreeable? Do you enjoy lathering up? Or do you rush through your bathing process? Why not take a little time and relish the experience? Touch and nourish your skin, your largest organ, with luscious-smelling oils and lotions. It only takes a moment.

Are your towels plush, soft, and inviting? How else can you linger and enjoy the sensations of touch?

Is your toothbrush soft and pliable or is it hard and rough? Is the toothpaste minty fresh and delicious so you brush for two full minutes and enjoy foaming up your mouth? Do you floss?

What are the colors surrounding your morning life? All whites? Sunshine yellows? Blues, greens, pinks, and reds?

Look around. What colors inspire you? How can you invite more pleasing colors into your morning?

As you prepare for your day, find things that will bring enjoyment to your morning rituals. If your surroundings do not bring you joy and gratification, consider changing or tweaking them to enhance your experience.

If you spend a good deal of time in your bathroom or dressing room, light a candle or burn incense as you bathe or dress. If you don't like artificial fragrances, buy yourself fresh flowers and plants to bring nature indoors.

Do you have windows that open out to your garden or yard? Open them in good weather and breathe in the natural air, taking deep purposeful breaths.

Resist turning on the TV or radio. If you live alone, listen to the quiet or the sounds of nature. If you live with others, engage in quiet conversation or agree to a quiet period until you have all gathered in a common area such as the breakfast nook.

Before you dress, stand in front of your closet and ask your body, *Body, what do you want to wear today?* This idea may sound silly. However, our bodies are wise, and when you are quiet and tune in, you will hear what your body truly desires to wear. It works every time.

As you dress, observe. Note the textures, the composition of the fabrics, the softness, the roughness, the warmth or the coolness. Take special note of the colors, the patterns. What do you discern about the clothes you put on your body? How does each piece of clothing make you feel?

When you clothe yourself in what your body tells you to wear, you feel fantastic. You feel like a million bucks. What happens when you feel like a million bucks? You make everyone you meet feel that way, too. Spread the feeling.

Look at yourself in the mirror. See your face. Smile.

Again, look at yourself and smile.

Look into your eyes and smile.

Say your name aloud, followed by "I love you." Say your name with "I thank you." Say your name and "I respect you."

Repeat this mantra three times.

Why?

This mantra, or chant, saying your name aloud followed by I love you, your name. I thank you, your name. I respect you, are from the incredible work of internationally acclaimed researcher Masaru Emoto. Emoto exposed water crystals to the energy of oral and written words in all languages and captured their images using a microscope. The water crystals exposed to words such as love, hope, trust, and joy are beautiful, symmetrical, magnificent art. However, the ones shown negative words like hate, fear, betrayal, and greed are disfigured.

In his book, *Love Thyself: The Message from Water III* (2004) Carlsbad, CA: Hay House, Inc., Emoto wrote,

> "The common language that the people of the world have been seeking is found in water crystals. Water speaks for what is in our mind. Water awakens the subconscious memory in each person. ... I now know why water is indispensable to the phenomenon of life, and why alternative therapies exist and why they're effective. Water helped me understand religion and prayer and gave me a clue to understanding the nature of energy.

It helped me understand the relationship between humanity and the cosmos. It gave me a clue to help me understand what dimensionality is. I could come one step closer to understanding the eternal theme of humanity that asks where we come from, why we are here, and what happens when we die. Thus, for the release of this, the third volume in my series of *The Message from Water*, I decided to choose what the world most urgently needs at present as a theme. That is, of course, the need to eliminate war and terrorism throughout the world. The theme I have chosen is 'prayer.' When I thought about it more deeply, I realized that prayer is most effectively sent when each person in the world raises their energy of love by imagining a scene where the peoples of the world are living in peace. I've been taught this through the process of asking water many questions. For this reason, the title of this book is 'Love Thyself.' First you must shine with positive, high-spirited vibrations, and be full of love. In order to do that, I think it's important to love, thank, and respect yourself. If that's the case, then each of those vibrations will be sent out into the world and the cosmos, and the great symphony of that harmonic vibration will wrap our planet in waves of love that serve to cherish our Heaven-granted lives. This is the message from water."[1]

After a few days, when you are more comfortable looking at yourself and repeating this love, thank, respect mantra, add this symbolic hand gesture (referred to as a mudra): Place your hands in a prayer position at your heart while saying the mantra. Sense the amplified power.

If you ever have difficulty falling asleep, or if you suffer from insomnia, chanting this mantra can help you fall asleep or fall back into slumber after waking.

---

[1] This mantra is more than an affirmation. When Masaru Emoto created this mantra, he learned that it heals, or cleans dirty and polluted water. The human body is roughly 55-60% water while the human brain and heart are 73% water, so this mantra can heal us physically on a cellular level, and it can heal us emotionally as well. I have witnessed it heal many of my clients – and when I say heal, I mean make them better and make them feel better. Some of my clients say it has cured their insomnia too. When they wake up in the middle of the night, they place their palms together at their heart, repeat the mantra, and go back to sleep right away. Using this mantra myself and with my clients, I can tell you it is powerful, and the results are nothing short of miraculous.

REFLECTIONS

What one thing will you do tomorrow morning to pay attention to you?

How can you awaken in a more mindful and pleasant manner?

Visit havenecarter.com/mindfulmoments/ to download your free, customized "[your name], I love you, [your name], I thank you, [your name], I respect you" mantra, these reflections and Chapter One resources, including a list of my favorite music and sounds for morning, my recommended meditation apps, and more.

Chapter Two
Mindful Cooking

Before you cook, ask your body, *Body, what do you want to eat for this meal?* Stand before your pantry, refrigerator, or countertop full of food and ask your body what it wants for nourishment. Wait and listen. Our bodies know better than our minds. Ask, wait, listen, and receive. The answer you get will be better than anything your mind might conjure.

Practice this same exercise as you make your grocery shopping list. Remember to make your list and shop for your food on a full stomach. Otherwise, you'll end up spending more than you intended and possibly making unhealthy choices—not shopping mindfully.

As you prepare your meal, pay attention to every aspect of the process. Take your time. Imagine it's your very first time seeing, touching, and smelling food. What if this was your first experience in a kitchen hearing all the noises associated with meal preparation: Water running, refrigerator door opening and closing, cabinets slamming, knives sharpening, and vegetables being chopped?

What if you organize your whole meal based solely on colors, textures, sizes, shapes, or smells? Get curious and explore your food choice tendencies. Explore. Play.

While washing your food, notice how it feels. Focus on the sensation of touch. How does the water feel on your hands? Is it hot, warm, cool, or cold? Is it a steady stream or does it pulse out of the faucet in spurts? Does the dirt easily wash off the vegetables or do you scrub? What else do you sense?

How does the food feel in your hands? Is it heavy or light? Smooth or rough, pebbly or hairy? What else can you appreciate?

How does it smell? Earthy? Fresh? Memories easily arise from aromas. Rest in a sweet memory for a moment before bringing yourself back to the present.

According to research, we humans can distinguish ten basic odors: fragrant, fruity, citrus, woody and resinous, chemical, sweet, minty and peppermint, toasted and nutty, pungent, and decayed. Combinations of these ten account for all the other fragrances, I suppose.

Breathe in the aromas of your food again. Do you detect anything new? Do you agree with the research?

What does your food look like? Look closer. Get curious and pick out the nuances.

Are you preparing meat, chicken, or fish? Take a moment to study it. Is it fatty, lean, bony? Amuse yourself with all the sensations. Close your eyes and play with your food!

It's time to chop, cut, or debone. What knife shall you choose? Feel the weight in your hand. Is it heavy or light? Inspect it for a moment. Is it shiny, sharp, dull? Hear the blade slice through the carrot, portabella mushroom, or yellow pepper and strike the wooden cutting board. What does it sound like in the beginning, middle, and end? Does it sound like music? It has a unique rhythm, doesn't it? Your personal beat.

See how your hands and fingers are connected to the knife. Are your fingers, hands, arms, and shoulders relaxed? Where are the tips of your fingers as you slice, cut, and dice?

Remember to spice it up. Add paprika, red pepper flakes, lemon pepper, garlic, lemon juice, turmeric, nutmeg, cinnamon, cloves, fresh mint, oregano, cumin, basil, or whatever is in your spice cabinet. Look at the different colors, grains, qualities, and consistencies. Open the jars and cans and sniff. Cut open the lemons and limes and take a whiff. Um... Bring the smells into your body. Breathe them in deeply.

Add a new spice to your shopping list each week. Explore the international aisle at your grocery store for interesting seasonings at great values. Search Asian, Mexican, and English markets in your area for exotic spices and new foods to eat.

Grow an herb garden and get creative.

Select your butters or oils—extra virgin olive, coconut, canola, walnut, grape seed—depending upon your usage, whether for cooked dishes or raw dishes. So many wonderful choices. Look at the varying weights and colors. Heed the degrees of lightness and darkness. Inhale the aromas, scents, and smells.

Choose pots, pans, spatulas, spoons, forks, and all your cooking accoutrements. Pay attention to why you want to use those items. Do you cook with the same items over and over when another may be better suited? Play with your pots and pans. Mix it up. Use a different one today. Try another one tomorrow.

As you cook, witness changes and identify variations. Stay connected to the cooking process and your senses.

While cooking, just cook. Give cooking 100% of your attention. Let all your efforts and all your attention rest on the art and science of cooking. Noticing all the sensations while cooking can be overwhelming. Break each sensation down—smell, taste, touch, sight, sound. Build them back up one at a time. Break them down again. Do your best.

Do you know how many different techniques you can try when cooking? Bake, barbecue, boil, braise, broil, casserole, fry, grill, microwave, poach, roast, sauté, scramble, steam, stir-fry, and more. Or are there?

Let your food rest before you eat. Let your mind rest too. Breathe. Take a break. Kiss your partner, your friend, or your dog. If alone, go to your mirror and kiss yourself. Say your 'I love you, I thank you, I respect you' mantra. Remember to say your name before each phrase.

Recapitulate this cooking experience. How did you feel? What was happening in your body? Were parts of your body tight, tense, relaxed, and loose? Which parts?

How was your breathing? Deep and relaxed or fast and shallow? Do you remember breathing?

What emotions arose? How many different sensations do you recall?

What was happening in your mind? Did memories surface? Were they bitter, sweet, or bittersweet?

Did your mind wander? Were you kind to yourself when you recognized it and brought yourself back into the moment?

Did you allow yourself to breathe space into the experience? Did you find some humor?

How did the food feel, look, smell, sound, and taste at the beginning, middle, and end of the process? You did nibble, didn't you?

REFLECTIONS

Describe your favorite food or meal to prepare and what happens in your body while you are preparing this meal. Or write about why you don't like to cook.

Recall your first experience in a kitchen while a meal was being prepared. Be specific.

To download these reflections and review Chapter Two resources, such as my favorite online shopping sites for great cooking tools and a few fun and easy recipes that are sure to please, visit havenecarter.com/mindfulmoments.

Chapter Three
Mindful Eating

"When you put a piece of bread into your mouth, chew only your bread and not your projects, worries, fears, and anger. This is the practice of mindfulness." **Thich Nhat Hanh**

As in Chapter Two, Mindful Cooking, before you eat, ask your body, *Body, what do you want to eat now?* Stand before your pantry, refrigerator, or countertop full of food and ask your body what it wants for nourishment. Wait and pay attention to what your body wants.

If in a restaurant, view the menu with your eyes in soft focus and ask your body, *Body, what do you want to eat now?* Scan the menu. Your eyes will guide you and focus on what it needs for nourishment and support. An open and clear mind and a little patience allow this practice to work like a charm each and every time.

In a restaurant, when other people are already eating or if there is a buffet, smell the array of aromas. See the colors, textures, and shapes of the foods. Ask your body what it wants to consume for nutrition, rejuvenation, and replenishment.

Drink an eight-ounce glass of water before each meal. A growling stomach is usually thirsty.

Do your best to refrain from drinking while chewing your food. Drink before and after you chew. Drinking water with your meal promotes easy digestion and nutrient absorption. If you drink wine or other alcoholic beverages with your meal, make sure you consume equal amounts of water and alcohol to avoid dehydration.

Serve and eat your meal on the *good* dishes, or the ones you save for company. Nourish your body and your soul. Today is a special occasion. Every day is special.

Before you pick up your utensils, behold the cuisine on your plate or in your bowl. Regard it in its totality and contemplate each component. Break down the details, examine the subtleties. Note all the colors. Scrutinize the differences, the contrasts, and the similarities. Smell the fragrances, spices, and bouquets.

Did you know our taste buds can distinguish six predominant tastes? Sweet, sour, salty, pungent, bitter, and astringent. Sweet is sugar, molasses, maple syrup, and honey; ripe fruit; grains, such as wheat, rice, oats, and corn; dairy products, particularly milk; meats, chicken, and fish; and, starchy vegetables like potatoes, sweet potatoes, parsnips, and squash. Sour is vinegar, citrus, berries, tamarind, tomatoes, and alcohol. Salty is salt, of course, meat and fish, eggs, and dairy, especially cheese. Pungent, or spicy, is onion, garlic, leeks, mustard, horseradish, wasabi, chilies, and most herbs and spices. Bitter is dark greens, such as spinach, broccoli, kale, and green cabbage, dark chocolate, coffee, and some spices like turmeric. And astringent is food rich in protein, such as avocado, raw broccoli, lentils, beans, and peas.

I'm getting hungry. Are you?

Which of the six distinct tastes is your favorite? Your least favorite?

Pick up your silverware and feel the coolness or warmth of the fork, knife, spoon, or chopsticks. Feel the weight of it in your hand. Have you ever noticed your fork before?

Dine. Eat slowly. Savor your food. Chew each bite thirty times before swallowing. This practice is mindful eating.

Be aware of the size of each bite on your fork or spoon. Make the next bite half that size.

Put your utensils down between each bite, chew your food, rest, and breathe. Eat another morsel. Your digestive system will thank you. You will enjoy your meal more. Your body will thank you. You will feel sated, but not stuffed after your meal. Your figure will write you a thank-you note!

Taste the flavors, spices, and seasonings. Distinguish the food from the spices. Feel the fork or spoon in contrast to the food on it.

While eating, only eat, don't do anything else. Enjoy the sensation of eating. Witness your own eating habits.

Slow down.

Breathe.

Use your napkin. Chew with your mouth closed. Don't talk while eating. Mind your manners.

♥

Enjoy it. See your food as if for the first time. Imagine you are an alien from another planet. What is this? Food?

Smell your food. Taste your food. Feel your food in your mouth. Hear yourself eat. I dare you not to giggle. Do your best.

Don't worry if you can't finish. You'll have leftovers.

Imagine all the tasty embellishments you can add to leftovers. (As if your delicious food needs them, right?) Chutney, hot sauce, salsa, avocado, fresh lemon juice, fresh rosemary, dill, yogurt, toasted almonds, or pine nuts. Yummy.

REFLECTIONS

Describe your experience of eating mindfully—eating while only eating, paying 100% attention to eating your food.

Complete this sentence:
My two favorite tastes are...

I like those two tastes best because...

Download these reflections and review Chapter Three resources, including a resource list of the six distinctive food tastes, a list of the most delicious foods from around the world, a chart of alkaline and acid foods, and information on why you should be paying attention at havenecarter.com/mindfulmoments.

Chapter Four
Mindful Driving

Make your car a place of comfort and well-being to create safe, easy, and agreeable driving experiences for yourself and your passengers.

Sit in the driver's seat and look around. Is your seat in the most secure location in relation to the steering wheel, the gas pedal, and the brake pedal? Make necessary adjustments. Play with the positions. How can you become more at ease?

Are your mirrors pointed so you have the best views? Can you see cars traveling around and behind you? Do you have blind spots? How's the perspective when you are reversing? Even if you have rear-end and side cameras, a smart car, you must still look both ways and behind you before moving.

♥

How does your car smell? Take a whiff.

Put a fresh-smelling satchel like lavender under a seat in your car to make it smell nice. Or you can hang a lemon-scented "tree" from your rearview mirror. No, please don't.

What color is your backseat upholstery? Is there an armrest for your backseat passengers? How well do you know your car or truck? Are your passengers comfortable back there? Have you ever ridden in your back seat? Get to know your vehicle.

First and foremost, when driving, drive. Just drive.

Your vehicle is a dangerous weapon when not treated cautiously. In a split second, it can kill you or someone else. Look down to adjust the thermostat for the air conditioning or heat and BAM! *What did I hit?*

Set your thermostat dials before you drive. Make adjustments at stoplights, stop signs, or pull over.

Look down to respond to that funny text, *I'm only writing LOL* and BAM! *What did I hit?*

Don't text and drive. Just drive.

There are fabulous smart phone applications that discourage the irresistible urge to answer texts while you're driving.

Look down to make that phone call, *I'm only pressing two buttons on my smart phone* and BAM! *What did I hit?*

Put your phone down and drive. Just drive.

Drive. See what is ahead and to the right, left, and behind. Begin again.

How do you feel when sitting in the driver's seat of your car? Do your buttocks sit evenly in the driver's seat? Are your muscles tense, tight, or relaxed and loose? How do your legs feel? Your feet? Your hips? Your knees? How do your shoulders, elbows, hands, and wrists feel? Are you relaxed? Or rigid and stiff? Inhale and exhale.

Notice your hands on the steering wheel. Are your hands at 10 and 2 o'clock? Are you lightly or tightly gripping the wheel? What does the steering wheel look like, feel like? Is it thin, thick, cold, warm?

Be aware of your tendencies and habits when in the driver's seat. Stay alert. Are you prepared for anything?

Do you remember the route you drove home from work yesterday? Where did you stop along the way? Take a new road tomorrow.

Watch which lane are you driving in. The left lane is for passing and faster moving traffic. Rule of thumb: If you are not passing, stay in the right lane.

Drive defensively. Pay attention to the traffic. Do other cars beep at you or flash their lights? What are the other cars around you doing? What are you doing?

Just drive.

Remember: Your vehicle is a dangerous weapon when not treated with caution.

If other drivers behave badly, do you react, respond, or breathe through it? Breathe. Life is too short.

Remember: There are 10,000 reasons why that other driver cut you off in traffic, sped past you at 90 mph, ran through that stop sign, didn't signal, was in the left lane for 40 miles, or tailgated you. He was rushing his child to the hospital, she was late for her wedding, she just found out it was stage 3, he just lost his job, her only son was just killed in a terrorist attack, or his wife was in labor—10,000 reasons, and you don't know why.

Sometimes we drive when we shouldn't. Do your best not to drive if you should not. Call a friend, taxi, or Uber/Lyft/Sidecar/Hailo/Curb/Juno (we don't want to leave anyone out, but I'm sure I have).

If you are the driver, just drive your car.

When you arrive at your destination, recapitulate the driving experience, the journey.

Turn on your headlights when you turn on your windshield wipers.

Stop at yellow lights. Yellow lights mean caution, prepare to stop. Stop while the light prepares to turn red. Yellow lights do not mean speed up and hurry through the intersection.

Stop at red lights. Red lights mean stop.

Stop signs mean stop. Stop at stop signs, and breathe. Then go.

Do not go as soon as the signal light turns green. Wait and look both ways before you proceed. Believe me, someone is driving along mindlessly (it was me) and might go through that red light.

Remember the 10,000 reasons? Well, I did not see the red light through my chemo-poisoned foggy brain. I really did not see it. As I passed underneath, I saw the green light signal to the left and thought, *Whoa, I'm going through a red light at 35 mph without a care in this world. What am I thinking about? Where am I?* I straightened up and looked around. Not a car or person in sight. *Whew!* Angels.

Reacquaint yourself with your state and local traffic laws. Become curious. Become open. Learn something new. Surprise yourself.

Take a new route to a familiar destination. Ride the road less traveled.

Drive like it's your first time behind the wheel. Remember that feeling? Remember that feeling.

REFLECTIONS

Without looking in your car or truck, describe its interior in detail.

Describe your last journey, the route you drove, what you encountered—other cars, traffic, the weather, delays or ease—everything you can remember.

Recall your driving test when you got your driver's license or permit.

Visit havenccarter.com/mindfulmoments to download these reflections and review Chapter Four resources, such as smart phone apps that block texts while you are driving and your state's latest driving and traffic laws website links.

Chapter Five
Mindful Interactions

"Mindfulness is the capacity of being there, fully present. ...the most precious gift you can give...is your true presence." **Thich Nhat Hanh**

Choose love. Fill your heart with love, and greet all others with love in your heart. Whether you are in person, on the phone, or interacting via email, come from a heart filled with love and your personal communications and interactions will flow with ease, grace, and honor.

When greeting someone, look into his or her eyes and smile. Think about it. When was the last time you gazed into your special someone's eyes? Do you look at the faces or into the eyes of the people you meet?

When greeting two or more people, take the time to look directly into each person's eyes and say hello. If meeting them for the first time, repeat their names to stamp them into your memory. Take your time. What is the hurry? When you slow down, it calms everyone around you and gives them permission to slow down too.

Listen to one another. Put away your phone, tablet, computer, game, paper, whatever, and give your full attention to your friend, partner, meeting participant. Give the person you are with 100% of your attention. If you cannot give your undivided attention to the one you are with, agree with him or her to each do your own thing while together.

Look at each other when speaking with one another.

Allow for space in your conversations. Take notice as another person speaks. Concentrate on what is said. Formulate your statement or next question after someone is finished speaking. You can even have a "filler" statement. "That's very interesting. I wonder if..." while you prepare your thoughts.

It's tempting to originate a clever comeback while someone else is still talking. However, if you are thinking while your friend, associate, or colleague is talking, you're not paying attention.

Honestly look at each other, and mindfully listen to each other.

Speak with intention and attention. Think before you speak. Are you reacting? Responding? Or creating what you want to state or ask?

Before you speak, remember the acronym THINK. Is it True? Is it Helpful? Is it Important? Is it Necessary? Is it Kind?

What's happening in your body as you listen to others? Pay attention to your body. Is it relaxed or tense? Are you sweating? How does your belly feel?

Meet others where they are. Get to know their style, their personality, and their language. Speak fluently with them. This approach is the ultimate in paying attention, in kindness.

How do you learn another's language? Curiosity. Interest. Ask questions.

Remember falling in love? How did you learn to speak that person's language? What did you do? What were you aware of? Every little thing, right? Bring this same wonderment and curiosity to every interaction.

If you are consistently misunderstood in communications, look inward. Examine yourself without judgment. Take note of your speaking habits and your body language tendencies. Do you interrupt others? Record a conversation and audit your listening skills.

Are you an arm crosser? Do you lean back in your chair or frown when listening intently? Think about what your facial expressions and body posture are signaling to others.

Do you write an email when a phone call is better suited?

Record yourself speaking on the phone with a friend and hear your tone, phrasing, and style. Are you mostly positive or negative?

Get with a trusted friend and video yourselves in conversation. Watch it together and regard how you speak, listen, and move. What do you hear and see? What are your habits and tendencies?

Be gentle and kind with yourself on this learning journey.

Practice mindfulness in all your daily interactions. Do you use the drive-through at the bank or the dry cleaner? Go inside next time and stay off your smart phone. Pretend you are a detective. Whenever you're in the coffee shop, dry cleaner, grocery store, or post office line, observe all the other people, workers, clients, customers, and patrons without judgment. Observe with curiosity.

If you see someone who appears frustrated, out of sorts, or just seems to be having a bad day, sit or stand in stillness and send divine and unconditional love to that person. If you see someone who appears lost, hurting, or confused, send agape love to the person, the situation, and the place before you choose whether to intervene from your heart.

Lift another's spirits. A smile, a warm "Hello, how are you?" can make a huge difference in another person's day. Like the ripples on the pond from the skipping stone, one sincere greeting can turn a frown upside down and smiles can spread throughout a whole community. How will you spread smiles today?

♥

Do you like to receive letters and cards in the mail? When was the last time you opened your mail box and found a letter?

Write a letter. Find a piece of stationary and write a letter the old-fashioned way. Do you have stationary? Remember the last time you wrote a letter? There was a time when people wrote tomes to one another to stay connected, a time when people went to visit an aunt or cousin and stayed for months. Of course, it took days and even weeks to travel here and there. Write your letter as an old-fashioned greeting to someone you haven't connected with in a while.

Fold the letter and put it in an envelope. Place a stamp carefully in the upper right-hand corner of the envelope. Address the envelope with your pen. Write your return address in the upper left-hand corner. Mail the letter. How does this process feel? Do any emotions arise? Are you surprised?

Enjoy the process.

Have no expectations.

Write another letter. And another.

Before phoning a company's customer service department for technical help or billing questions, sit in stillness for a minute or two. Plant both feet on the floor. Focus on your breath, settle your nerves, and quiet your mind. Now visualize a lovely customer service representative who is kind, considerate, and helpful. One who does everything possible to resolve your issues. Hear your own nice voice introducing yourself as well as patiently and calmly explaining the situation and asking for assistance. Listen as all is resolved and you both say thank you several times. Everything goes much better than you could have ever imagined. What else is possible? How can it get even better than this?

Imagine getting everything you want or something better. You will. You deserve it. Believe it.

REFLECTIONS

Complete this sentence:
The last time I looked someone in the face and directly the eyes, I felt...
Physically:

Emotionally:

Mentally:

Spiritually:

When you listen to someone, how do you usually compose your face and body?

Describe your speaking tone and style when on the phone. Are you mostly positive or mostly negative? Do you speak slowly and clearly or quickly and indistinctly?

To review Chapter Five resources, including a downloadable THINK mini-poster and inspirational quotes from some of my favorite teachers, and download these reflections, visit havenecarter.com/mindfulmoments.

Chapter Six
Mindful Relationships

"The most precious gift you can give to the one you love is your true presence." **Thich Nhat Hanh**

Mind the baggage you bring to your relationships. Be careful not to project your baggage onto your loved ones.

Each day, several times a day, focus your intention to pay attention to your loved ones.

Rather than using the Golden Rule, "Do unto others as you would have them do unto you," instead do unto others as they wish to have done unto them. What you wish to do for them may not be what they wish to have done for them. Find out what others want, and then deliver.

Be curious. Ask questions. Never make assumptions. Keep an open mind. Find out what others wish.

People change. Do your best not to allow stale habits to stagnate your closest relationships, but do create fresh habits that strengthen and grow your relationships and allow them to flourish.

Everyday ask yourself, *What can I do for the people I love today to show them I love them?*

Surprise your loved ones every day. Write a love poem. Clean his golf shoes. Take a shower together. Bake cupcakes with your children or grandkids. Fill her gas tank. Order dinner in. Read her a story. Take the family out! Bring him flowers. What else can you do to surprise the people you care about? It only takes a moment.

In your closest relationship, ask yourself:

> *Is it*
> *I want your love*

or
I want to give you my love?

Is it
I want you
or
I want to give you the best of me?

Is it
I want your time
or
I want to give you my time?

Is it
I want your everything
or
I want to give you everything your heart desires?

Is it
I want you to take care of me
or
I want to take care of you?

What happened as you read the passage above? Did any emotions arise? Did anything shift in your physical body? Any memories stir? Witness without judgment.

Discover your loved one's love language and speak it with him or her every day. Dr. Gary Chapman, author of *The 5 Love Languages*, says we speak five love languages: Words of Affirmation, Acts of Service, Receiving Gifts, Quality Time, and Physical Touch. Most of us enjoy all these at one time or another. Who wouldn't, right? One or two of them are more dominant within us than the others. What is your primary love language? What are the love languages of those you love?

Consider the words you speak. Do they affirm or criticize?

Be aware of your acts of service. Do you serve with a loving and grateful heart without expecting anything in return? Or do you think of service as a duty? Do you expect acknowledgment and reward for your service?

Notice whether you give freely. If you don't receive a *thank you*, what emotions bubble up?

How do you and your loved ones spend your time together? Are you engaged with one another? Disengaged? What do you want this time together to look like? Imagine your perfect day together. Make it happen.

Play with physical touch. Tickle. Hold hands. Hug. Kiss. Do you want more touch or less touch in your life? Talk with your partner about it.

Engage, explore, and enliven your life with the five love languages.

Ask for what you want, and ask others what they want and need.

Listen without commenting. Listen without expectations. Respond thoughtfully and mindfully.

Spend time in stillness together.

Take walks without talking. Leave the earbuds at home. Detect something new about the person you love. Resist telling yourself stories about what you see. Simply observe and rest in it.

Now notice something else interesting about this person and find beauty in it. Whatever it is, there is loveliness in it. There is something to appreciate in it all. Tell him or her about it in specific detail. Her bewitching crooked finger that makes you giggle, his one-arched eyebrow and pirate-scary stare, his flat feet drumming his unique rhythm when he walks across the hardwood floor, her graying temples that make her eyes shine.

Upon meeting her future husband John, my friend Monica said to him in awe, "You have a Spock ear!" He replied, "Yes, and as soon as I save enough money, I'm going to have the other one fixed to match it." A match made in heaven.

Beauty lies in the eye of the beholder, and perception is everything. Remember the splendor and the magnificence in the little and big things about the people you love. So often those closest to us make us crazy and we forget or we stop appreciating the idiosyncrasies we used to adore. Flip it. Whenever your love does that *thing*, marvel at his or her brilliance instead of dismissing or dissing it.

Remember, love is an action first. My mother used to tell me to love—the action— especially when I did not feel the emotion. The action begets the emotion.

The more you act with love, the more you feel love. The more you love (act), the more you love (feel).

Love is the answer no matter the question.

Choose love. Choose to love.

REFLECTIONS

Complete these sentences:

I am choosing love by...

The thing that drives me crazy about my partner is...

I'm going to flip it by...

Download these reflections and Chapter Six resources, such as "Six Questions to Ask Your Partner Regularly," the New York Times article, "36 Questions that Lead to Love," and my "Is it" poem at havenecarter.com/mindfulmoments.

Chapter Seven
Mindful Living

Affirm your life's purpose in a mantra, affirmation, mudra, or movement each day. Keep this focus and intention as your guiding light, your anchor in all you are and all you do.

Before you do, remember to be. Be here now. Be in the moment.

We are human *beings*, not doings.

Each day, several times a day, set the intention to pay attention.

Discover something new every day.

Are you curious and want to discover more? Pretend you are a visitor in your own home. What do you see, hear, smell? What else?

How might you choose to engage, to be more in your own life?

Notice the expansion and contraction of time and space. When in your life does time or space seem to expand? Contract? How can you expand time in your life? How can you expand the space?

Reflect. Do you live from a heart of abundance and love or scarcity and fear? A life based in love and abundance is open, reflective, heart-based, inclusive, mindful, nonjudgmental, creative, expansive, curious, thoughtful, active, somatic, focused, appreciative, patient, and kind.

Be here now.

Breathe in and out. Quiet your mind.

No judgments or stories. No worries about yesterday or tomorrow. Only here and now.

Sit. In. Stillness.

Smell the moment.

Taste the moment.

Feel the moment.

Hear the moment.

See the moment.

Sit in stillness.

In the quiet. Amid the chaos.

Begin again.

Allow your flower to blossom.

Notice the unfolding. Do not interfere. Observe.

Let the players perform the drama.

Listen. Do not react, and do not respond. Continue to create your life.

Listen to your body, emotions, mind, and spirit. Listen, and give them what they ask for.

Listen, and move gently with love and humor.

Listen, and release your emotions and heal.

Listen, and let your spirit soar.

Love yourself first.

Love all others.

Be compassionate with yourself.

Be compassionate with all beings.

Begin again.

REFLECTIONS

How will you create your life based in abundance?

How will you live a mindful life?

To download Chapter Seven resources, including two free guided meditations and these reflections, visit havenecarter.com/mindfulmoments.

GRATITUDE

To my clients, who prodded me to write "all this stuff" down, you all are my teachers, and I am most appreciative.

To my editor, Martha Hayes, I am so grateful for your insight, perception, mountain of knowledge, resources, and love for this project and me. Thank you.

Thank you, Lee Heinrich. You seeded this publishing thing for me, and you continue to encourage me. I am forever grateful and honored to be under your smart and caring wing.

Tremendous appreciation, joy, loving-kindness, and gratitude to my teacher Ranga Premaratna. Ranga, your peaceful, easy, and calm spirit guides me daily. Thank for your patience, teachings, communications, and perceptions.

Blessings and appreciation to Andrea Snyder for gifting the subtitle for this baby and for introducing me to Nancy, who led me to new paths and pastures.

Thank you to all the readers of my drafts who provided incredible feedback and concise criticism with love and care. I could always count on you, and I appreciate you all for wanting to help me make everything better. I could not have completed this project without you.

Mother, thanks for modeling so many wonderful things for me, especially the love of books and reading.

Awesome Chix, thank you for your strong broad shoulders of support and your encouraging words and incredible wisdom.

Monica, thanks for believing in me. Keep pushing.

To my best teachers—Lucien and Gypsy—thanks for your constant support, patience, and belief in me, especially when I didn't have them for myself.

And finally, Professor Jim Shumaker. I remember timidly standing at your door. It was a few weeks before my college graduation in 1982, and I was fishing for direction, affirmation, a compliment maybe, something. It took every bit of courage I had to ask you, "Do you think I can write?" You looked at me, that forever twinkle in your eye, and said, "There's only one way to find out. Write." Thirty-four years later, I am beginning again. I sense your spirit dancing and playing with mine. Thanks.

Notes

Grateful acknowledgement for the use of quoted text and speech from my teachers, all used with written permission.

Dr. Ranga Premaratna, used with permission.

Teijo Munnich, used with permission.

Thich Nhat Hanh, *The Art of Power* © (2007) New York, NY: Harper Collins, *Work: How to Find Joy and Meaning in Each Hour of the Day* © (2012) Berkeley, CA: Parallax Press, *True Love: A Practice for Awakening the Heart* © (2011) Boston, MA: Shambhala, used with permission.

Piero Ferrucci, *The Power of Kindness: The Unexpected Benefits of Leading a Compassionate Life* © (2007) New York, NY: Jeremy P. Tarcher/Penguin, used with permission.

Debbie Rosas, Nia Technique ®, used with permission.

Rosie Osmun, "Why Electronics Don't Belong in Your Bedroom" Lifehack Blog, used with permission.

Joshua Becker, "11 Reasons to Create a Technology-Free Bedroom" Becoming Minimalist Blog, used with permission.

Masaru Emoto, *Love Thyself: The Message from Water III* © (2004) Carlsbad, CA: Hay House Inc., used with permission.

Dr. Gary Chapman, *The 5 Love Languages* © (2015) Chicago, IL: Northfield Publishing, used with permission. Visit www.5lovelanguages.com to take the official love languages quiz/assessment.

What Haven's Clients Say

"Working with Haven is changing my life. If you need something to help bring you in, to explore the inner you, and be better than your best, consider working with Haven.

Mica

"Haven's skills with meditation and Reiki seem to come from an authentically spiritual place; but I have found they are beneficial to both my business and personal life, in tangible ways. Over a corporate career, I have worked with a number of professional performance coaches; but Haven's approach is unique in my experience. She obviously does not employ a formula that she delivers by rote; she clearly intuits what is needed in each distinct situation and offers tools that can lead toward a solution."

Elaine

"Haven's Mindful Meditation sessions were a turnaround for me on my approach to meditation. I have now successfully inserted a mindful, peaceful time almost daily."

Lynne

"Haven embodies the very essence of the compassion she teaches during her meditation classes. Her teaching style is relatable, natural, loving, and reassuring. I am forever grateful to her for the profound impact she has had and continues to have on my life."

Julie

"Haven Carter is a healer! I have experienced her gifts through Reiki, Nia, and her amazing compassion meditations. She is a vessel that transmits Light and Love. I am deeply grateful to have experienced the beautiful essence of Haven in my life."

Kate

"Having lots of stress in my life, I decided to try guided meditation with Haven to take the calming, spiritual, and joyful aspects of Nia to another level. Although Haven has given me excellent tools for meditation on my own, I find that I really need weekly guided meditation with her as she has enabled me to decrease stress and to develop a mindfulness and calmness that was missing in my life. Haven is the BEST!"

Martha

"I am thankful to Haven for getting me started on a meditation habit. When I'm feeling stressed and distracted, I take a break to meditate. I always come back more focused and ready to get things done. And strangely, my business has increased since I started meditating."

Maria

Connect with Haven

Website: havenecarter.com

Follow her on Twitter: @HavenECarter

Friend her on Facebook:
www.facebook.com/haven.carter

Connect on LinkedIn:
www.linkedin.com/in/havencarter

www.ingramcontent.com/pod-product-compliance
Lightning Source LLC
Chambersburg PA
CBHW071630040426
42452CB00009B/1571